Illustrations

The work reproduced in the first part of this book is by students of the Ruhr Teachers' Advanced Training College, Dortmund Section, and the author. Other illustrations are from the Pelikan Archives and the collection of the Department of Art Education, Ruhr Teachers' Advanced Training College, Dortmund Section. A further source was the Kothe-Marxmeier school, Trantenroth, Bochum. Rembrandt's drawing "The Quack' is reproduced by kind permission of the State Museum of the Preussischer Kulturbesitz Foundation. The drawing 'Rashomon' by Sakai Hoitsu was published in *Meisterwerke aussereuropäischer Malerei: Chinesische und Japanische Malerei* by Werner Speiser and is reproduced here by courtesy of Safari-Verlag, Berlin.

Sponsored by the Günther Wagner Pelikan-Werke, Hannover; and Koh-I-Noor, Inc., 100 North Street, Bloomsbury, New Jersey 08804

German edition © 1968 Otto Maier Verlag, Ravensburg, Germany.
English Translation Copyright © 1969 by Reinhold Book Corporation.
Library of Congress Catalog Card Number 78-83388.

Printed and bound in Italy.
Published in the United States of America by Van Nostrand Reinhold Company,
450 West 33rd Street, New York, N.Y. 10001.

Foreword

Inks, blots and stains, scratchy pointed nibs, upset ink pots, black fingers — all these are closely associated in our minds.

India ink is black, ordinary ink is often blue. There is also red ink, a source of great worry to us in our business ledgers and personal budgets. Generally our knowledge of the materials does not go very far. We write in ink, draw in india ink. The process is as simple as could be: the writing or drawing implement is dipped in the little pot and the line is made on the paper. Such tools and operations are hardly designed to fire our technical imagination — which is why the use of india ink and other inks in schools remains so restricted in spite of the versatility of these materials.

There is an additional feature which discourages many: once a line has been drawn (particularly in india ink) it is not very easily obliterated. You can erase pencil, wipe off charcoal, paint over paints. But ink eats into the paper and is indestructible evidence of an effort, successful or otherwise. However, this permanence is also of great educational value.

Ink is an ancient feature of human culture. The civilization of East Asia is unthinkable without india ink. Who could have written the papyrus scrolls of the Old Testament without ink? The composition and preparation of inks may have changed through the centuries, but they are still kept, as in the dim past, in little pots or jars. Originally brown ink, 'sepia', was made of the substance the cuttlefish ejects when it feels itself threatened. Many other types of ink were plant extracts: blue black ink was made of the juice of oakgalls in which iron filings were dissolved; india ink was based on fine lampblack and water-soluble resins. Today the chemical industry can replace almost all the ancient pigments with artificial substances. However, many inks are still prepared in exactly the same way as they were by their inventors.

There is a basic difference between india ink and other inks. India ink, once dry, is insoluble in water. Other inks, unless they are of a special kind, remain water-soluble even after thorough drying. Both kinds of ink exist in many variations and colours and have the most varied uses. Almost all can be used for creative work, provided they are used correctly, allowances are made for their peculiarities, and their capabilities are fully explored.

The purpose of this book is to show how much can be done with inks if they are intelligently applied.

Rembrandt: 'The Quack'. Photograph by Steinkopf
Sakai Hoitsu: 'Rashomon'

How to use india ink

When should you start using india ink? Is it a material for adults only? Success in a medium depends on how you start. A clumsy hand cannot get any results from the simplest methods. And it is much easier to learn when you are young than when you are old. When a child is 'old enough' for 'difficult materials', it is usually too late to teach him much. So india ink is perfectly suitable for children.

It is possible to paint very exactly and very 'beautifully' with india ink. A child whose creative urge is encouraged may produce 'beautiful pictures', and the teacher may congratulate himself on having brought out a talent. However, more important than the production of beautiful pictures is allowing a child to experience the creation of his own world of pictures, which is richer than a mere copy of reality could ever be. Any creative composition is an enrichment of our surroundings.

Most of the materials are very cheap. They have common everyday uses. Their artistic value lies in handling them, gaining experience with them, learning their possibilities and limitations. For every material has potentialities and teaches us to think creatively — think like a creator. Every material offers fresh ideas to the original mind, provided it is approached in the right spirit.

Many people think they can work away like a master who knows everything about his material; they are surprised and annoyed when they fail. Many others think that it is sufficient to work with the material within the limits of convention; they are disappointed when their results are only mediocre. The material has to be studied in detail; and you have to start at the beginning.

Anyone can make an ink blot
All you have to do is put a drop of
ink on a piece of paper, then fold
the paper, and you have produced
a blot print. No two of these blot
prints are alike.

A blot can be altered, made
larger, longer, wider; but chance
will always play a large part.

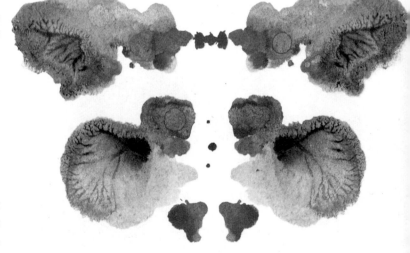

Let us now add coloured india ink
and other inks. We shall at once
produce shapes of strange beauty.

6

A big, fat blob invites you to let it run on the paper — and to blow it about vigorously. You may even use a straw to produce some effects. This blowing on india-ink spots and lines is a wonderful starting point for much creative activity.

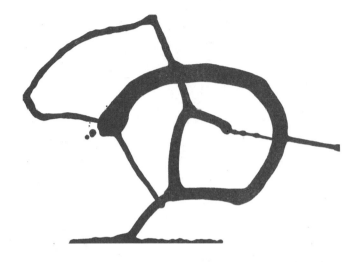

Grasses and trees seem to grow;

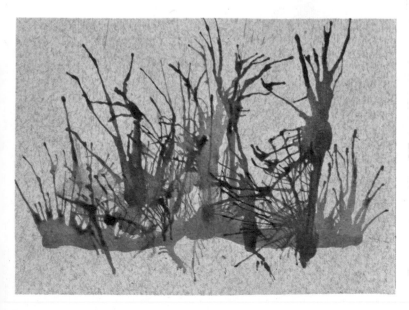

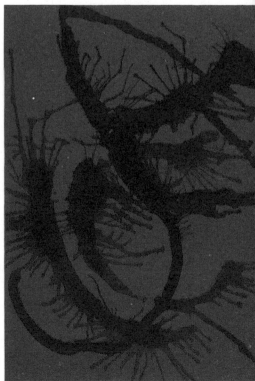

hair, eyebrows and bushy mous-
taches appear on robbers and
pirates.

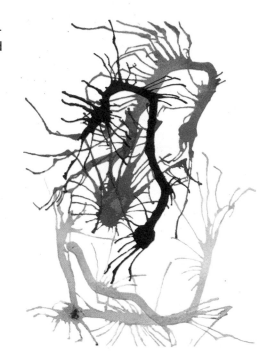

Here, too, various kinds of ink can
be used. Even the simplest materials can have a great effect.

You can extend the treatment of
the ink drop, the blot and the
simple thick line. First apply them
vigorously near the bottom edge of
a sheet of drawing paper. Then
cover the paper with another sheet
and with the edge of your hand — a
lino-printing roller is also eminently suitable — squeeze the india
ink between the two sheets to-
wards the upper edge. When the

two sheets of paper are pulled apart, shapes and shades of sometimes astonishing delicacy occur.

Or deposit a pool of india ink on a sheet of glass and press a sheet of paper on it. Here too the effect will be enhanced by the use of various inks.

Drawing implements: wooden stick, stump, painting rag

We have just been talking about the pointed nib and the brush as drawing implements. But at first these tools are difficult to handle. Start by drawing with a piece of wood split off a piece of firewood, or with a wooden toothpick. It is quite incredible what you can do with such a simple tool. Fine, delicate lines can be drawn with its edge, wide lines with the side. There is no end to the intermediate possibilities.

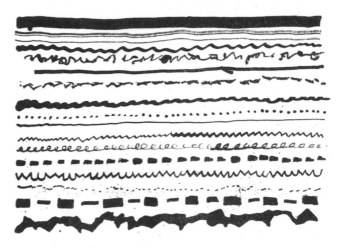

The wood soaks up india ink or any other kind of ink. The first line is deep black, but the colour fades progressively, becoming more and more grey. Working with these grey values creates a special graphic appeal.

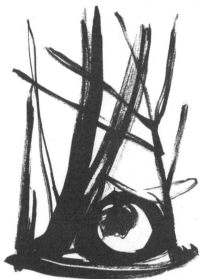

Now roll a piece of paper quite tightly, producing a paper stump, which will soak up a great deal of india ink.

You can paint at once with the soaking-wet stump, or wait until the india ink has completely penetrated the paper. If you wait, the paper will yield the india ink only slightly so that the grey values dominate.

And now, of course, we combine the wooden stick and the paper stump.

But we have still to mention another important tool: the simple painting rag. You can draw with it, wipe with it, stipple with it. It is quite impossible to work in a 'pretty' fashion with the painting rag. Here we have a technique for the large format, designed to encourage small painters to 'think big'.

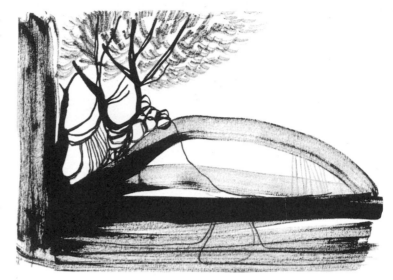

Grey shades with water and india inks

You can extend this technique slightly by diluting india ink with water, making several concentrations. This provides you with a number of shades of grey in addition to deep black. (Something obvious must be mentioned here: this thinning method is of course a possibility with almost all other techniques. The wash-off techniques may be an exception; they will be described below. They are based on fully saturated blacks or blues.)

With such graduated grey shades it is now possible to 'build up' a picture, letting it dry between steps.

Brush and india ink

Back to the simple, undiluted ink. We are describing black india ink, but any other ink can be used in exactly the same way. The most popular tool is the brush; any size and type will do.

Strokes with a flat-ended brush will be a little coarse and clumsy although, used in the right way, the brush produces versatile results.

The pointed sable brush, which is like the tool used in the Orient, is more congenial to india ink. You can fully bring out the charm and expressive force of india ink only with the sable brush and the reed, which we are going to describe below. Try to hold the sable brush as the Chinese do: by the top of the handle, between thumb and index finger.

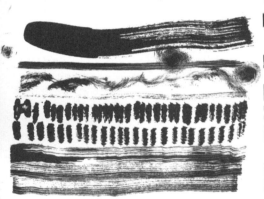

You can write with this sable brush 'dancing' and 'swinging' across the paper.

(We must point out that all

14

brushes must be thoroughly cleaned after use, as a matter of routine. With india ink this is particularly important; although water-soluble when wet, dried india ink cannot be removed from the brush.)

If you do not mind getting your fingers dirty, try the following method. Fill the brush with india ink, wipe it well, and squeeze it flat between thumb and index finger. It will spread out like a little fan, and each fine tip of hair will carry the ink individually. You can produce lines of spider-web fineness as with no other implement. To continue this work, all you have to do is to dip the hair tips gently into a blob of india ink.

If you are patient enough you can produce the most delicate screen structures.

The steel pen

The steel pen is the most common of all ink implements — we generally write with it. If we use it for drawing, the lines generally look as if we were still writing. When we write, what we wish to convey becomes more important than the graphic method of putting it on paper. This makes the line dull, threadlike, nondescript. But this is by no means the limit of the steel pen's possibilities.

Anybody can draw with a pencil. To draw with a pen seems more special — especially to primary-school children. Of course precautions are necessary when a child uses india ink or he will get himself very dirty. But these precautions can be the occasion for useful training; the child must in any case learn how to be neat and careful as he grows up. Most eight-year-olds are quite capable of

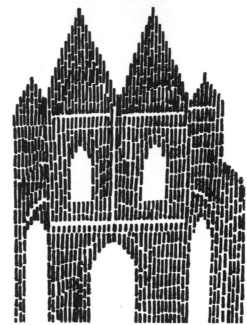

using pen and india ink without disaster.

Certain effects are easy with the broad-nibbed pen which is really designed for large script.

You can do more than draw lines with the steel pen; you need only explore its potentialities.

Pen drawing as we usually think of it starts with the fine, pointed drawing pen, which is made of particularly thin, elastic steel, and registers every pressure of the hand.

One can make delicate, even lines,

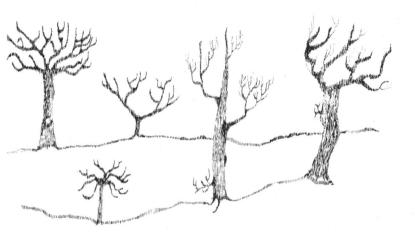

but can also vary them between thin and thick.

Thick, fine and ultrafine points are also made. They can produce a variety of textures.

The reed

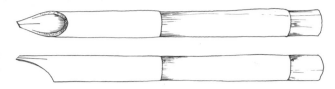

The reed is the tool of the masters. It fits snugly in the hand and meets the most exacting artistic demands.

The implement can be cut from reeds growing on the banks of almost any lake or river. The best time for cutting is September, when the reeds are hard and strong. A reed can be prepared for drawing as soon as it is well dried out. Cut it with a sharp knife so that it does not splinter or tear. This requires some practice.

The variety of lines that can be drawn with this instrument is almost unlimited. The reed permits sweeping, swinging strokes, but also delicate, fine drawing in soft shades from black to grey. It is a tool for both meticulous and bold scripts.

eines hispano— moresken schautellers

As with colours, variations with tools are many. You can use painting rag and reed on one occasion, reed and drawing pen on the next. Your own experiments will open up many new possibilities and lead to inventions of your own.

Some things only certain inks can do

Most techniques are suitable for any kind of ink, ordinary or india. But some can be executed only with india ink or only with ordinary ink. Thus, an additive colour build-up is possible only with the transparent blue ink or with the coloured india inks.

When you cross a brush stroke of blue ink with a second stroke, the colour strengths will add up where the strokes overlap.

If a stroke of blue india ink is crossed by one of yellow, or red, or green, you obtain a colour mixture, as can be demonstrated with coloured transparent paper.

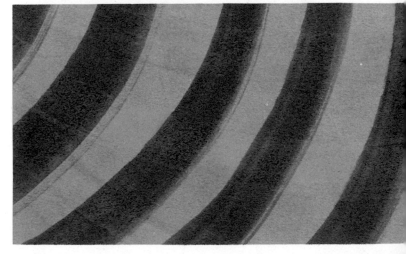

Or an inked background wiped on with a painting rag can be wiped over again after it has dried. This will change or strengthen the colour.

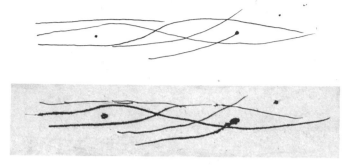

penetrate. The ink remains on top and dries with a gloss. If the line, blot or shape is rather thick, the india ink will crack on the paper. The dried india ink, which 'lies' on the surface of the art paper, can be scraped off with a penknife or an etching needle. This characteristic lends itself admirably to many possibilities of composition.

The exact opposite happens with Japanese rice paper. Every drop of india ink or any other ink im-

Paper

Use good-quality white cartridge paper, as wood-free as possible. On good paper the lines stay strictly where you want them. On unsized, wood-pulp paper, lines will run, so that you cannot control the effect.

Of course, you may want a 'wrong' effect. Occasionally it is rewarding to give yourself over to chance when you apply ink to paper. You often find that obvious faults can be made use of for deliberate effects.

Two types of paper offer special qualities to the worker in ink: glossy-coated art paper, and the Japanese rice tissue paper (the latter has the disadvantage of being rather expensive).

Art paper has a dense compact surface which india ink can hardly

mediately sinks into the paper. Rice paper is available in several types, all suitable for printing. Usually they are strongly absorbent, which affects the appearance of the lines. Some papers are particularly fibrous, which results in characteristic structures of lines or shapes.

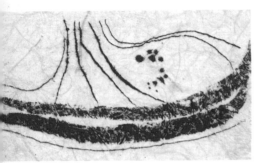 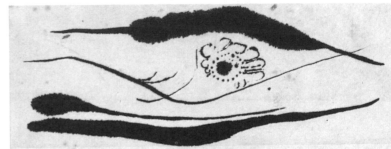

Sprayed india ink

We are still dealing with the question of how india ink and other inks are applied to the paper. We have not yet mentioned the spray method. India ink is put into a tube of fixative and sprayed on to the paper in fine droplets like a black mist. The fixative tube is the ideal tool for the pattern spray technique.

You need not start with cut-out patterns right away. You can arrange nails, pebbles, leaves, pliers, keys, scissors or any other small objects in an orderly manner on the table and spray them with india ink. Naturally the india ink can also

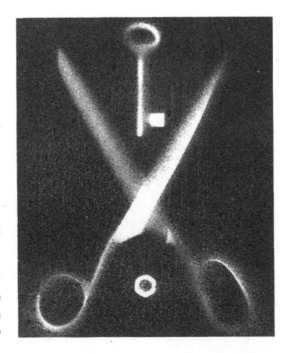

be flicked from a painter's brush if no fixative tube is available. Wash the india ink off sprayed objects before it dries.

Patterns are best cut from cardboard previously waterproofed with linseed oil, floor polish, candle wax or a wax crayon. You can spray several times, rearranging the patterns after each spraying so that in the end a rich variety of shades is obtained.

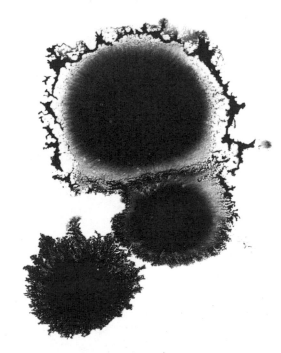

Work on damp paper

Up till now we have discussed techniques in which india ink alone was actively employed with various drawing implements. Now we add water to vary its effect. Wet-in-wet, a well-known method of poster painting, opens up new and very specific possibilities to india ink. Let us again start at the beginning, with the blot.

An india-ink blot falls on damp

paper. First one, then several. Already, without your intervention, the india ink and the water do their own 'creative' work. The blots radiate like sunbursts and suggest compositions. You can make a formal arrangement of radiating points or, by combining the blots with other techniques, one that represents concrete features. Naturally, the paper must be well dried before you add sharp lines.

Because a line of india ink on damp paper also has a will of its own, you can use a line-blot combination.

Another technique that involves water produces surprising effects

and is very simple. On dry paper, paint an area with coloured ink, using a broad brush. Then scratch

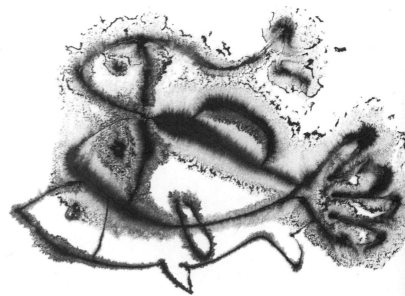

lines in the paper through the ink while it is still wet with a pointed object (needle, etching needle, nail file, scissors, etc.). The ink will immediately penetrate the scratches in the paper and produce a deep-toned line. The ink painting could be left like this, but it will be more effective if the surplus ink is washed off the paper before it has had time to penetrate too deeply. If for some reason or other washing under the tap is not possible — no running water in the room, too large a class, or children who are too young — use blotting paper; newspaper or waste paper will also do the trick.

This technique can be applied in several stages, with india ink of different colours.

Simple collages

The last technique will have taught the child that scratched paper greedily soaks up ink. This suggests another technique.

25

Shapes or rough figures are torn from white cartridge paper and glued to another sheet. The torn edges will absorb india ink or other inks particularly strongly. The whole collage is liberally covered with ink, then washed. The torn edges produce the design.

Now take your experiment a step further by using papers of different absorption capacities. Tear out shapes, arrange them on the base sheet and glue them down, brush on india ink, then wash. You will obtain a collage of different shades. You can do this with white paper, but also with any coloured paper at hand.

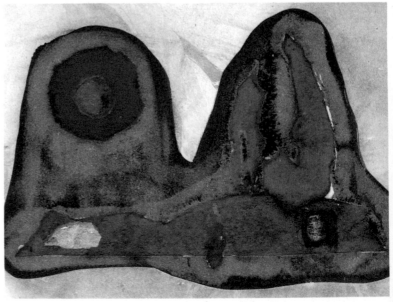

Wax batik and wax etching

A special version of wax etching is wax batik, which can be pursued very successfully with india ink. Rub cartridge paper vigorously with a white paraffin candle, then scratch the paper deeply with a pointed implement. You know that scratched paper absorbs india ink greedily. The film of wax along the scratch prevents the india ink from spreading. The scratches are now filled with india ink.

All you have to do to remove the superfluous india ink is to hold the wax etching under a running tap. Sometimes it is enough merely to wipe it with a dry rag.

Every now and then you may want to leave the ink on the paper where it has dried on the wax.

What is possible with the ordinary household candle can of course also be done with wax crayons of different colours. However, here washing is recommended, since india ink adheres to the crayon strokes.

Thus we have learned a number of washing-off techniques. Various materials prevent liquid dyes from penetrating a base — in this case the paper. Wax is one of them, as you have just seen.

Make a drawing on paper with a paraffin candle, then cover it with broad strokes of india or other ink. After a little time wash the india

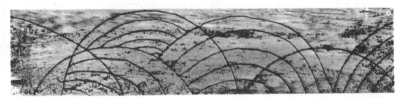

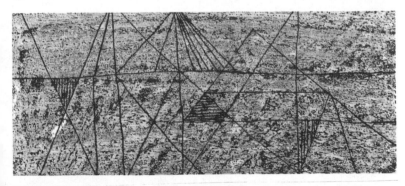

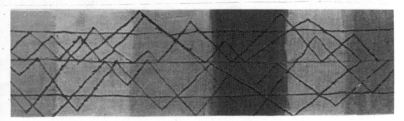

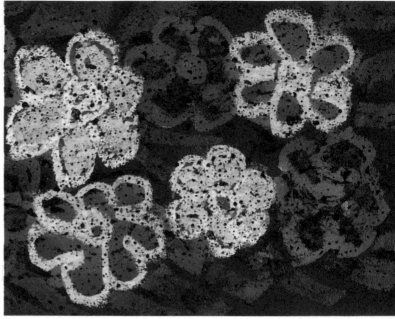

ink off under a running tap. The paper under the candle stroke will remain white. Depending on the quality of the candle, washing the sheet with water may not be absolutely necessary; a dry painting rag may be adequate for dabbing or wiping the ink off.

The colour drawing here was started with yellow india ink. Red ordinary ink, blue ordinary ink, and finally black india ink were applied one after the other; at each stage the paper was washed off, dried, and covered with another drawing. All traces and shapes that were to remain unchanged were carefully covered with wax before the next stage.

Split-off and wash-off

Poster white can be used like wax. If it is applied to the paper almost undiluted, even directly from the tube, it will dry matt and, exactly like the wax, prevent india ink from penetrating the paper. The paper is then densely sprayed or painted with india ink.

Two alternatives are now open: wet and dry.

The wet wash-off technique is similar to the candle technique, except that you must take care to wash off even the smallest trace of poster white to prevent the appearance of white blotches on the paper. You will obtain a simple, white drawing. It is not difficult to

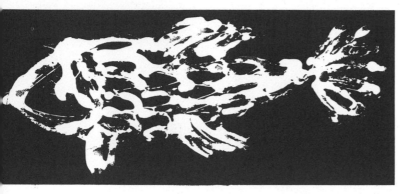

achieve this, as you will see.

The dry method is called the split-off technique. Its pictorial effect is decidedly more interesting and fruitful than that of the wet technique. The poster white must be completely dry. The india ink is liberally applied on top of it and also allowed to dry thoroughly. The india ink will split off all by itself. You can aid this process with a penknife, if it seems necessary to help the pictorial composition. You should not be too optimistic with this rather special technique. It does not always work out as you would like.

Another technique, which really leads to satisfactory results, can be derived from the split-off technique: making pictures by scraping.

For this purpose the entire surface of the paper must be prepared with a copious amount of poster white which is allowed to dry, then covered with india ink, which is also allowed to dry. After that, the picture can be scraped with sharp implements.

There is another very simple scratch technique in which india-inked paper is scratched with a pointed nib. The scratching exposes the white paper underneath.

You have seen that poster white prevents india ink from penetrating the paper. To a certain extent the other poster paints also have this property. But their covering power is not quite as great, and so after the top coat of india ink is applied and washed off, all the colours will have an interesting grey tinge. Here the effect is largely the result of chance, which of course can produce bad pictures as well as good ones.

Glue and ink

Various pastes and glues applied to paper and allowed to dry will protect the paper against india ink. The wash-off process is the same. Here is another special technique. Cartridge paper is covered with white paste, such as is used in schools and libraries. A drawing is made on it with the brush handle. The dried sheet is covered with india ink and allowed to dry again. Then the india ink is washed off. Special graphically interesting and attractive results are possible with gum arabic. The picture is painted on a white sheet with gum arabic.

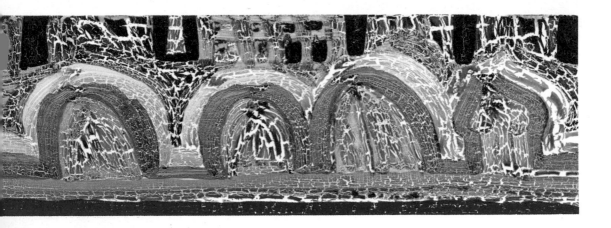

When the gum drawing is dry, it is painted over with india ink, which immediately cracks above all the gummed portions. Naturally washing-off is omitted here.

Finally, you can directly draw on paper from a tube of quick-drying household cement.

This can be done on tracing paper, and the cement is then covered with ink. The picture is not washed off. The special effect is produced by transmitted light.

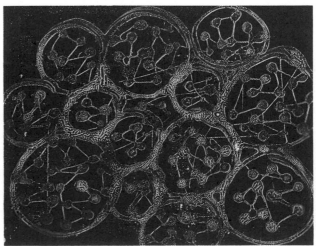

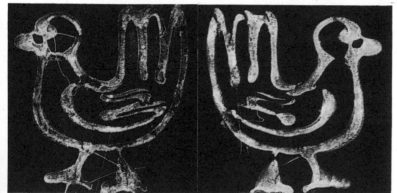

Printing techniques

We shall now discuss printing with adhesives. This can be less wasteful than, for example, drawing with household cement on paper, using up a great deal of cement for a single drawing. The stroke of cement stands out very sharply from the paper. If you cover it with a second sheet of paper, you obtain a print, which can be treated further in various ways.

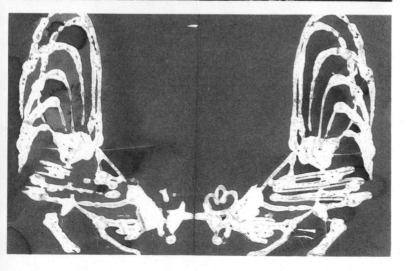

Or you can try a folding print, essentially a blot printing with household cement, to produce symmetrical shapes.

If you use waterproof white household glue instead of cement, you obtain quite a special effect, which is seen in the folded ornamental print shown here. The effect is produced when the folded glue drawing is allowed to dry thoroughly, then covered with ink and washed off comparatively rapidly. It is difficult to give any times for this process; you must experiment.

The glue-printing and wash-off technique is in any case very fruitful. It is very old; it was used, for instance, by the Westphalian blue printers, who printed with a paste of flour, pipe clay and other ingredients with blocks on fabric. The fabric was subsequently dyed in an indigo bath.

One of our illustrations shows patterns of the edge of a rolled corrugated-cardboard sheet, the other patterns of the rim of a cigarette box. Both objects were dipped in white paste, and printed. This was followed by the application of india ink and washing off. This technique is called blind printing.

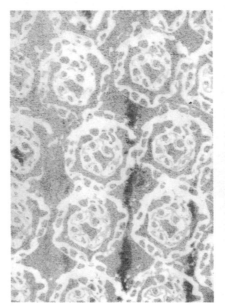
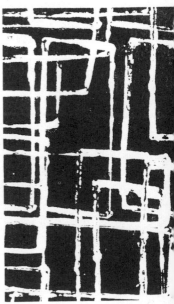

a

b

The most advanced technique suitable for schools is the lino blind print, in which liquid glue is applied to the block with a printing roller. The stages after printing correspond to the blind-printing technique described above: allow to dry, ink, then wash off (b). Experimenting is necessary here. Every liquid glue has special properties which must be thoroughly explored. Here, too, white glue produces special effects (a). Blind printing with lino blocks is of educational importance even beyond the technical interest: the simplest type of lino printing is white-line printing. With the technique demonstrated here the pupil can produce negative prints and at the same time see the positive effect of his block. Blind printing reverses the effects.

Let us return to pattern printing. This time you do not use india ink for spraying and stippling, but glue. The india ink is applied afterwards. Again, the normal effect is reversed. The positive pattern produces positive shapes, and the negative pattern negative shapes.

You could continue with this method almost indefinitely; the possibilities of variations are by no means exhausted. After all, inks are an ideal material for experimenting.

Remember that wood can be stained with india ink, and that the stain is water-resistant. Such treatment shows up the grain particularly well.

Fountain pens

We must not end this discussion without mentioning india-ink fountain pens.

These implements are designed for technical drawing, where straight, precise lines of constant width and neutral aspect are essential. They really come into their own on the drawing board.

This does not mean that they can-not be used artistically. They are eminently suitable for hatching and shading, creative construc-tion, and geometrical repetitive treatment of a subject. The most varied drawing tools are available, and they can easily be exchanged even during work. This ensures a wide variety of effects. The ex-amples here demonstrate some of the many possibilities.

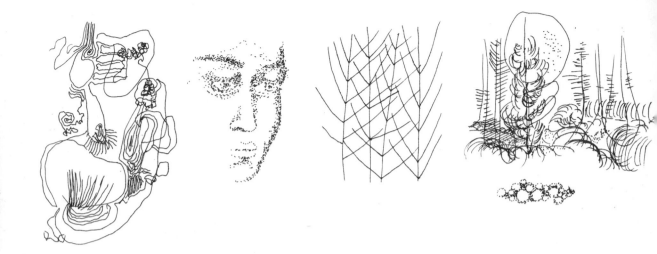

Playing and experimenting with ink

With india inks and other inks, play and experiment are closely related. But is it proper to play in school? Playing is a widely discussed subject at the moment. It is supposed to relax, to liberate and to establish contacts. Yet it is opposed by some serious educators, who fear that play activities divert the student from responsible work and education in the narrower sense.

But nature, which is certainly more cleverly designed than any school that can be imagined, has arranged that play is man's first means of obtaining knowledge about his environment. And thus education has its best chance of success when it is based on the human capacity for play.

Play requires a freedom from unnecessary restrictions, a lively intellect and a healthy mental attitude. Any stinting of these requirements reduces the ability to play, and any reduction of the ability to play impedes the progress of education.

Small wonder that 'playing' is an important part of art education. In the child, play is a serious form of work and experiment.

Why do we discuss play in connection with ink? Well, consider the ink blot.

From certain points of view, an ink blot has little to commend it to the classroom. It is a waste of time and material. It is 'dirt'. It results from carelessness, if not from deliberate malice.

But children are magically attracted to a blot. They dip a finger, a stick, a piece of rag in it, wipe it, even give it a definite shape. Children have the gift of transforming many an object that appears to us grown-ups a futile triviality. They are still full of curiosity. They still are something the grown-up does not even know how to define: they still are creative.

Now let us offer the ink blot as a subject: 'Let's see what an ink blot can do!' An experiment, then? Of course the grown-up experimenter would proceed in a grown-up way. He would sit down and think: 'How do I tackle the problem? What does ink consist of? What can I, therefore, expect it to do?' He would then go on to check his speculations, acting them out in experiments.

This is what we should expect from the adult, and even from the adolescent. The results of such investigations can then be utilized for new creative possibilities.

The child 'works' differently. He plays: he approaches the subject 'blot' in a way that gains him empirical knowledge, teaches him everything that the adult finds through experiment. The child experiences by means of his creative activities. He does not yet distinguish between experience, appreciation, knowledge and application.

Practical application teaches the child that the useless blot can do a lot of things. It can run, leaving a track. It can be forced into a direction that he has chosen. If he holds the sheet obliquely, or taps it on the table, the drop or blot will run wherever he wants. The child will concentrate on his task, whether it is imposed by the teacher or by himself: this blot is to become a rectangle, a spiral, a snake, a house, a face.

Play and problem — a relaxed and occasionally also a deep mental involvement, real participation. We could use this method ourselves during many a serious project we undertake.

Or the child blows on the ink blot. He has been asked to do it. If he blows at the blot slowly, it moves. If he blows strongly from the side, the blot bursts into fine splashes, and it will look like a comet, grass, a tree, a beard. The child can make a star-spangled sky, or a meadow, or a whole pirate with a beard, bushy eyebrows, and hair blown all over his head.

Finally he can blow straight from above. This drives the fine threads of india ink apart in all directions and produces a star on the paper, as impressive as any that could be made with a drawing pen.

Now he folds the paper over the blot, making a blot print — a picture produced by the blot and chance together. Magic shapes appear, animals, flowers, landscapes, all occupying the child's imagination and stimulating him to new inventions. The richness of forms, presented to the child in a way he can understand, is inexhaustible. He mentally digests these forms, expands on them, interprets them, gives them names, takes possession of them.

What the child is doing is more than foolish dabbling. 'Trivialities' teach the child something about his environment. To respect trivialities is a great virtue. This respect includes consideration, paying attention, observation and the examination of effects for their causes.

This play can be extended. Up to now it has consisted of playing with the material, getting acquainted with it, finding a way into the world in order to participate in it. But what does this ink blot achieve for aesthetic education? First the eye and the hand, individually and together, are sensitized. The child is taught and teaches himself to observe phenomena of creativeness, which he will later meet in works of art. He learns at an early stage to use — even if not to comprehend — part of the spiritual language of the work of art.

Aesthetic shapes grow under the hands of children at play. While they experience action and procedure, it dawns on them how astonishing, how wonderful they are.

There is another form of play. The teacher gives the pupil a task to be performed with specific objects, but with an unpredictable result.

He may say: 'Here is a line as long as your index finger; the second line is only half as long. You may draw them as thick or thin as you like. They may intersect or join to form angles. You can take as many lines of each kind as you wish — but they must always be one length or the other, and they must always meet at right angles.'

All the children play the same game with the same rules. Yet each is left to go his own, still unknown way. The 'order' laid down by the teacher, the vertical-horizontal, is the only certainty. And the teacher considers 'orderliness' such an important creative force that he wants it to become second nature

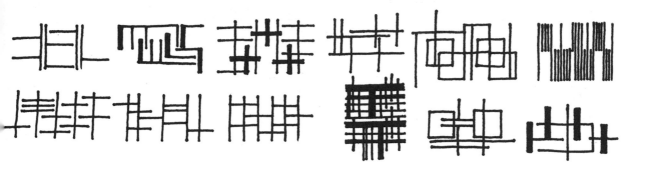

— consciously or subconsciously — to the child.

In spite of the rules, this game allows the child to make his own decisions and provokes him into constructive thought. The scope of this decision is wide, no matter how narrowly the subject may have been delineated.

This still leaves the techniques to be discussed. How do we do it? There are techniques galore: drawing with the steel pen, the reed, the wooden stick; printing with the edge of a sheet of cardboard; direct application of india ink; the wash-off technique; wax etching; wax batik. Chance may furtively enter the rules of the game and introduce attractions of its own.

What has happened? The child learns to put up with the limitations of his medium and to make the best of the modest means at his command. He orients himself by laid-down rules and invents new ones. He experiences order as a creative, picture-producing phenomenon. Again the eye is being sensitized. But now the intellect, too, participates; it has to think, to assess. An order that is creative, not merely conscientious, is set up, an order that is aesthetically balanced. The translation of such tasks into aleatory processes — that is, techniques whose actions produce chance results — opens up the mind. If the same subject is used for drawing on damp paper the child acquires a new experience of chance and learns, when he becomes conscious of it, to gain control of it and to accord it its due place in his creative vocabulary.

This makes it a play activity with a very serious basis. It furthers the powers of imagination and creative anticipation.

We were 'dealing with material' or 'investigating through playing' when we experimented with the ink blot. With the vertical and horizontal lines we encountered

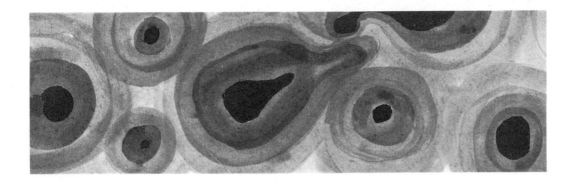

the 'arrangement of elements' or 'games with rules'.

Next we try 'application of recognized principles' or 'achievement play', which starts from knowledge already acquired.

This activity demands abilities which can be taken for granted on the strength of what has been taught before. For example, suppose the child has learned about the graduated dilution and, therefore, transformation into grey of black ink. He is asked to produce a variety of grey steps and produce an optimum effect through a basic composition that is as richly disposed as possible. The one task thus makes two demands at once: a technical, manual one and a compositional, arranging one. Essential to both is a measurable variety: variety of shades and variety of composition.

What happens? Again all the children have the same start. However, the decisive point now is to make progress by broadening the scope of the work. This is a contest that requires involvement, grasp, ability and also industry. The teacher could propose: 'We are making a map showing the altitudes of an imaginary mountain region. The highest peaks are marked with the undiluted black ink, and the lowest valleys with the most diluted ink.'

This problem will reveal that there can be meaningful limits to the variety of shades and arrangements. This places this play activity, too, beyond the mechanistic and in the creative range.

Nor are these the only principles of play. Let us mention one more in conclusion: the 'optical gift' or 'expansion play'. All the children start from the same object, given to them by the teacher. Here it could be a coarse blackboard sponge, slightly moistened with india ink and given to each child in turn to print on his sheet of drawing paper. This print is the central feature of a composition for which all the possible techniques and materials are made available. The problem is to use this central feature to organise the whole sheet graphically.

Here each child must make decisions for himself. The basic object presented must be explored, its fundamental structure grasped, and variations of it invented. This encourages in the child concentration and the technically correct use of media.

Thus inks and the tools used with them are suitable playthings from which much can be learned. Playing with them will teach the children how to play correctly with them. They will then also be able to work with them.

Reproduced on the following pages are a number of works in india ink and other inks by students responding to specific tasks presented to them.

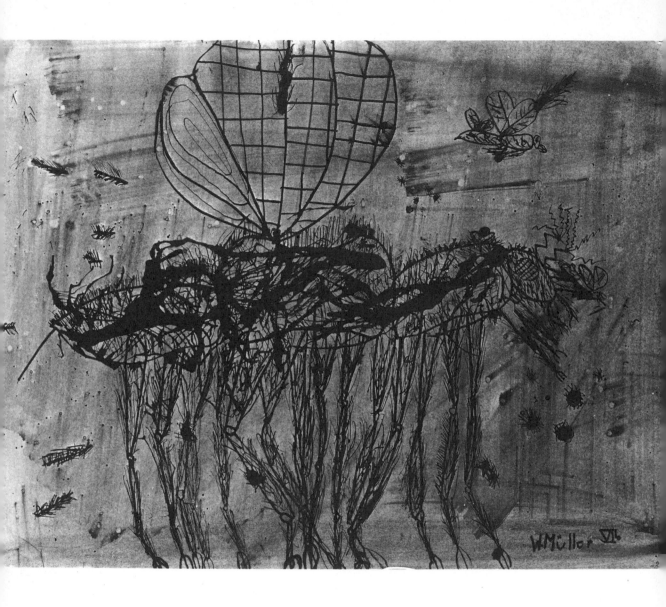

'The Big Grey Fly' (boy, 11). The whole surface of the paper was first dyed grey with a painting rag dipped into diluted india ink. Ink blots were placed on this background, then the boy blew on them, elaborated them with a pen, and interpreted them as the picture of an insect (see p. 8).

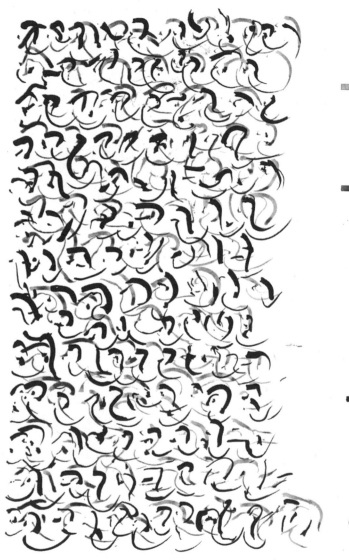

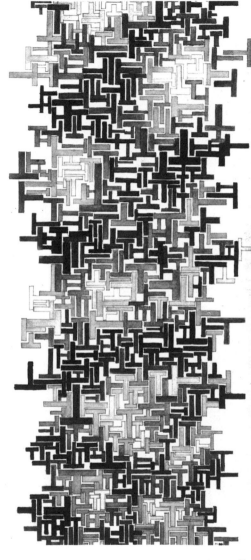

'Imaginary Handwriting' (girl, 14). 'Writing' with a brush. Undiluted and diluted india ink.

Formal order based on the element T (girl, 14). India ink of various dilutions. For technique, see pp. 13-14.

'Oriental City.' Pen drawing with
an ordinary pen and india ink.

46

'Waiting for the Bus' (boy, 11).
'Continuous-line' drawing with a
fountain pen.

'Shells on the Beach' (boy, 10). Two solutions of the same subject. The decorative interpretation with strong lines contrasts with the ornamental and descriptive-detail drawing, in which many small shapes are arranged around two large shells.

'Dragobi', a monster (boy, 12).
Blue ordinary ink and fountain
pen.

Pen drawing with black india ink.
The artist succeeded in organizing
the picture area by using various
forms of lines and arrangements of
lines.

Pen drawing with white india ink.

Pen drawing. The uniform structure based on parallels is broken up
by different directions and con-
densations of lines.

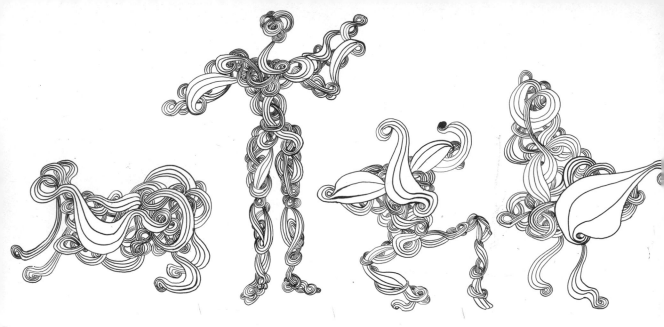

'Knot Figures' (girl, 15). Composition with parallel lines. Steel pen and india ink.

Design for a greeting card (girl, 15). India ink and pointed drawing pen.

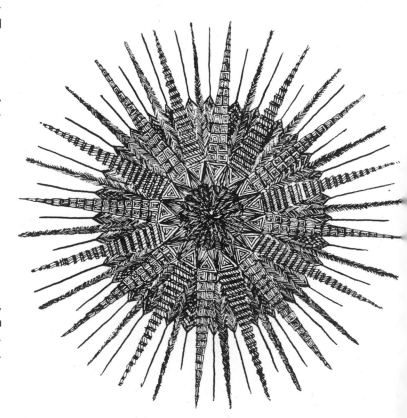

Facing page: 'Ship in Port' (boy, 18). Pen drawing with black india ink. A piece of work which combines much narrative flair, technical grasp and perspective vision.

52

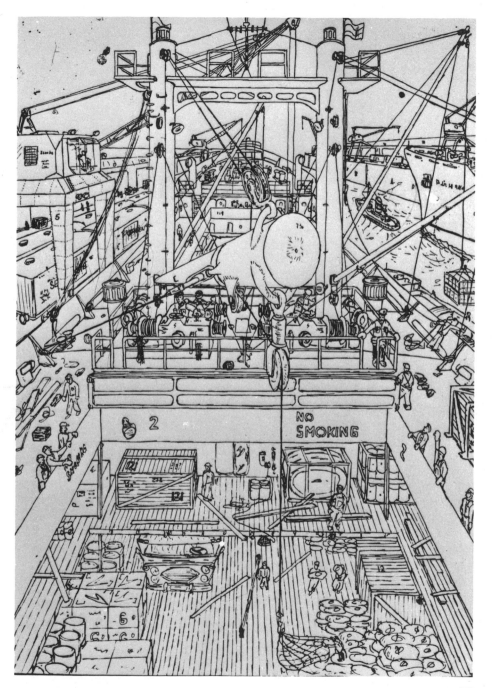

'Songbirds on a Sunflower.' Pen drawing. The various features are distinguished by a variation of their textures (see p. 37).

54

'Ants Attacking Caterpillars.' Black india ink and writing pen. Here the identical shape of the ants becomes the structural element, arranged according to distribution and concentration.

Steel pen and black india ink. The paper was first thoroughly damped. On the wet ground the india ink 'flowered' into mossy structures.

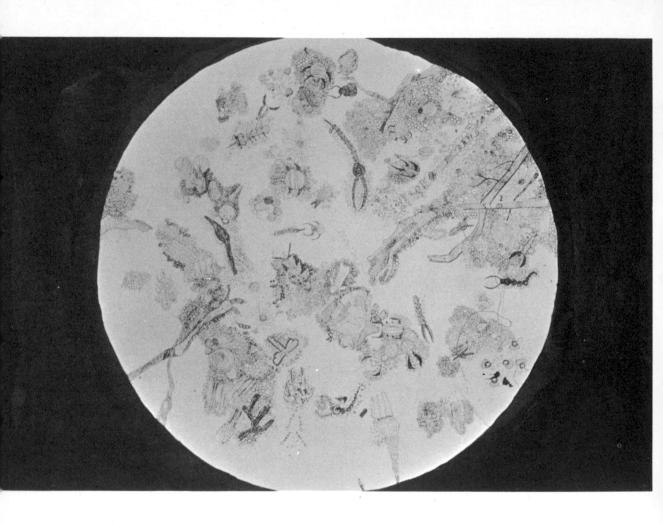

'Look through the Microscope'
(girl, 12). India-ink drawing with
the fine drawing pen. For technique, see p. 17.

'View from an Aeroplane' (girl, 15). This picture is composed entirely of dots. The special effect is created by a change from thick to thin dots and different arrangements of the dots. For technique, see p. 37.

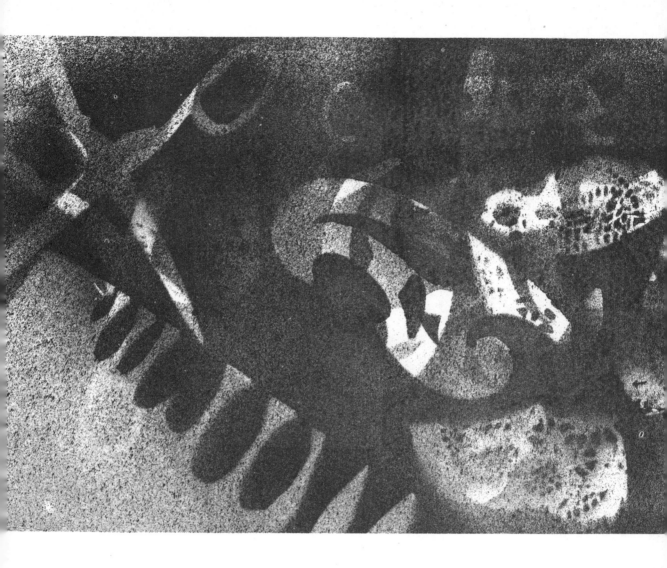

Facing page: spraying technique with india ink (girl, 12). Masks, progressively larger from the centre outwards, were placed on the paper. For technique, see p. 22.

Another example of spraying technique with india ink (girl, 12). Scissors, French curves, a key, a doily, and scraps of cardboard were used as patterns. For technique, see p. 22.

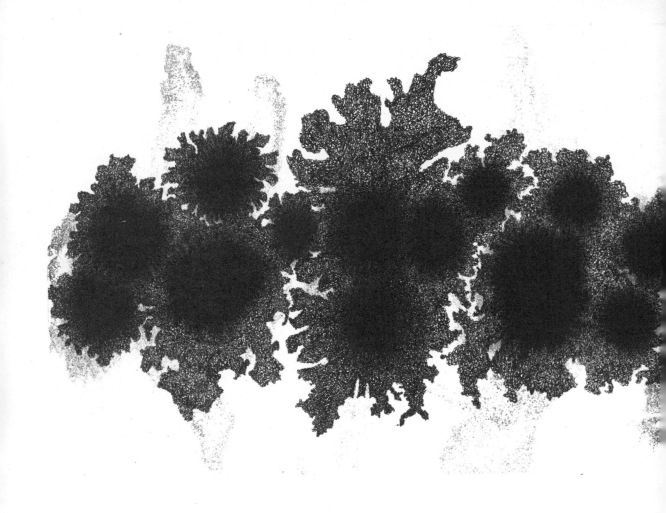

This composition is based on
india-ink blots on damp paper
(girl, 11). The dried sheets were
finished with a fine drawing pen.

60

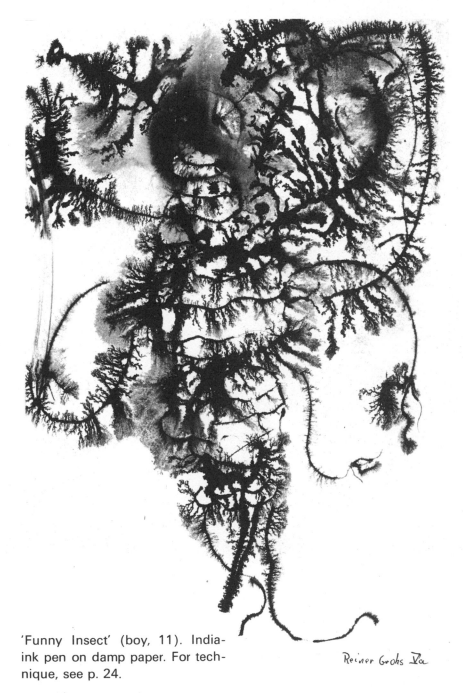

'Funny Insect' (boy, 11). India-
ink pen on damp paper. For technique, see p. 24.

Reiner Grohs IVa

'The Flower Garden' (boy, 10). The flowers were painted with poster paints. After complete drying they were covered with black india ink, which was washed off under the water tap (see p. 30).

'Trees in the Enchanted Forest'
(boy, 10). Coloured wax crayon
drawing. The trees were left blank.
Eventually the whole was painted
over with blue-black india ink.

'Rooster.' All colours were applied to the white paper with wax crayon, followed by black india ink, which penetrated the paper wherever it was not covered with wax.

'Houses round the Market Square' (girl, 8). White paste and black india ink. For technique, see p. 31.

'At the Meeting' (boy, 11). A picture in india-ink wash-off technique. Whatever was to remain white in the final picture was covered with water-soluble glue. A fine brush or steel pen was used for the fine writing lines. For technique, see p. 31.

'Walls of a Ruined Castle' (girl, 12). Drawing with gum arabic and black india ink. For technique, see p. 32.

Geometrical pattern (girl, 15). Points were marked at equal distances along the upper and the lower edges of the sheet and were connected with india ink and drawing pen.

Facing page, left: structural composition by concentration and linear arrangement of identical elements (girl, 13). Steel pen and india ink.

Facing page, right: linear and vertical arrangement with concentration through superimposition of the elements (girl, 10). The basic element is a U.

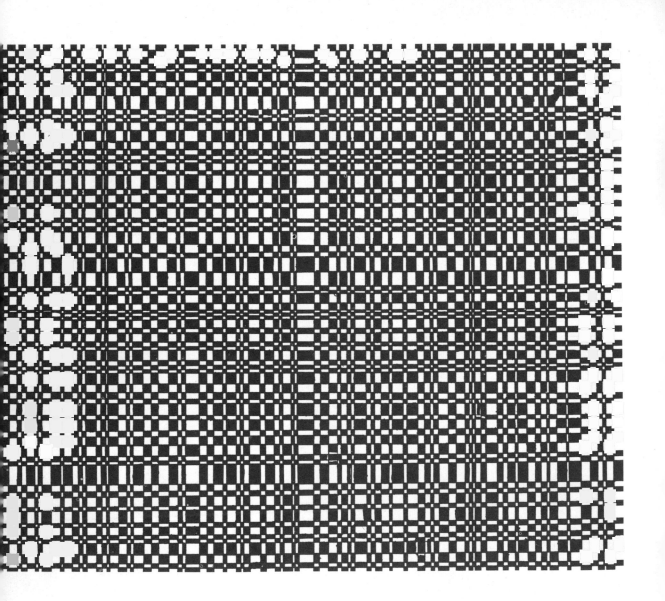

Repetitive variation of the chess-
board (girl, 15). Positive and
negative alternately dominate.

Index